WHERE HAVE ALL THE PANDAS GONE?

Questions and Answers About Endangered Animals

BY MELVIN AND GILDA BERGER
ILLUSTRATED BY JIM EFFLER

CONTENTS

Introduction • 3

LAND ANIMALS IN TROUBLE • 6

BIRDS IN TROUBLE • 18

WATER ANIMALS IN TROUBLE • 32

Index • 48

About the Authors and Illustrator • 48

KEY TO ABBREVIATIONS

ha = hectare
kg = kilogram
km = kilometer/kilometre
km² = square kilometer/kilometre
kph = kilometers/kilometres per hour
m = meter/metre

ISBN 0-439-26669-6

Book design by David Saylor and Nancy Sabato

10 9 8 7 6 5 4 3 2 1   01 02 03 04 05

Printed in the U.S.A.   08
First printing, October 2001

Expert reader: Diane Lynch, Fish and Wildlife Bioligist
Endangered Species Division, U.S. Fish and Wildlife Service, Hadley, MA

The animals on the cover are pandas.
The title page shows brown pelicans and their nest.
A tiger cub is on page 3.

For Max, who loves animals in the wild
— M. AND G. BERGER

For my wife, Debbie
— J. EFFLER

INTRODUCTION

What are endangered animals?

Animals that are in immediate danger of dying out, or becoming extinct. Another category, threatened animals, are low in number but with little danger of disappearing. Many endangered animals are familiar: pandas, gorillas, and tigers on land; eagles, condors, and pelicans in the air; whales, sea turtles, and crocodiles in the water. But there are thousands more that you may not have heard of. And some may become extinct before they are even discovered.

Were animals always endangered?

Yes. Animal extinction is a natural part of life. Dinosaurs were probably driven to extinction when an asteroid struck our planet some 65 million years ago. Giant mammoths died out about 10,000 years ago when the Ice Age ended and the world's climate grew warmer. But the situation is different today. Different species, or kinds, of animals are now disappearing about 1,000 times faster than ever before!

Why are more animals endangered today?

The growing number of people on Earth. As the population rises, people occupy or destroy animals' habitats—the places where the animals live. Without habitats, the animals cannot find enough food to eat or places to raise their young. Overhunting often leaves too few animals for survival. And pollution of the land and water drives ever more animals onto the endangered species list.

What is the endangered species list?

The names of animal and plant species in danger of disappearing. In the United States, two government agencies, the U.S. Fish and Wildlife Service and the National Marine Fisheries Service, prepare the list with the help of scientists. Experts count or estimate the number of individuals in species that are low in number or rapidly losing members.

From time to time, the list changes. Sometimes, a species gains members and is removed from the list. But you can be sure that every animal on the endangered list is in serious trouble.

Why is the endangered species list important?

It names all animals that need protection. The Endangered Species Act, a law passed in 1973, forbids killing, trapping, or harming animals on the list in any way.

The list of endangered animals also leads governments to set aside parks and refuges. Here the endangered animals can live and find food in safety. Zoos and research centers mate animals that are very close to extinction. This is called captive breeding. Often, the hope is to return the offspring to the wild.

What is the future of endangered animals?

Hopeful. Several laws and programs seem to be working. The numbers of certain endangered animals, including alligators, bald eagles, and pelicans, are increasing. The peregrine falcon is coming back in some new areas. The fate of many others is in our hands.

Let's hope—and help!

Melvin Berger   Gilda Berger

Newly hatched green sea turtles

LAND ANIMALS IN TROUBLE

Where have all the pandas gone?

From the bamboo forests of China—to near extinction. Today, there are only about 1,000 giant pandas left in the entire world. (The smaller red pandas are not in danger.)

Giant pandas are very fussy eaters. They feed almost entirely on bamboo. In fact, these chubby animals have an extra thumblike "finger" on their front paws just for grabbing the shoots, leaves, and stems off bamboo plants.

An adult giant panda weighs as much as 350 pounds (160 kg) and is up to 5 feet (1.5 m) long! Each one eats up to 44 pounds (20 kg) of bamboo every day. When the bamboo is gone in one area, the pandas must move through the forest to find more.

Why are pandas endangered?

Over the years, people leveled whole bamboo forests to make room for homes and farms. Ranchers cleared large areas for grazing their cattle. Workers cut bamboo to manufacture many products, from furniture to fishing poles. Without bamboo forests, many giant pandas starved to death.

Also, poachers capture giant pandas for their beautiful fur. Some of these illegal hunters can live a whole *year* from the sale of a single giant panda skin.

Are people saving the pandas?

Yes. In China, the government set up forest refuges for the giant pandas. Here they have plenty of bamboo and are safe from poachers. Scientists around the world also practice captive breeding. The first panda born in the United States came in August 1999 when a panda cub was born at the San Diego Zoo.

Giant panda

Mountain gorillas

Where have all the mountain gorillas gone?

From their habitats on the mountain slopes of Africa—to near extinction. Today, there are only about 600 of these magnificent creatures roaming the rain forests of that continent. (Lowland gorillas, however, are still safe.)

Mountain gorillas are the largest of the apes. A full-grown male may weigh 450 pounds (204 kg) and stand 6 feet (1.8 m) tall. Most mountain gorillas live in groups as large as 30. All day long, they feed on the leaves, bark, and fruit of the trees. Just before dark they build a nest on the ground or in low tree branches. Every night, they build a new nest. Each group needs lots of room for sleeping and wandering. A typical home range for a group of mountain gorillas is about 15 square miles (39 km^2), or the size of a small town!

Why are mountain gorillas endangered?

Humans are taking over their habitat. Year after year, workers clear vast tracts of land for farms, ranches, and factories. Also, loggers cut down huge numbers of forest trees for lumber. The destruction leaves the mountain gorillas with too little room to gather food and raise their families.

Poachers capture live mountain gorillas for sale to zoos. Hunters kill the gorillas for sport. Some people hunt them for food. And some traders kill the gorillas and cut off their heads and hands to sell to tourists as souvenirs.

Are people saving the mountain gorillas?

Yes, by working to preserve their habitat. One forest reserve in Africa is home to half the world's population of mountain gorillas. These gorillas are doing well in the protected area, where they are safe from poachers.

Where have all the monkeys gone?

From their homes in the wild—to near extinction. You can find the names of some 20 species of monkeys on the list of endangered animals. One species, for example, is the golden lion tamarin. Only 400 of these animals remain in their native habitat, the tropical rain forests near the city of Rio de Janeiro in Brazil.

About the size of squirrels, golden lion tamarins are named for their long, yellow-orange, silky manes. The monkeys spend their entire lives in trees searching for fruit, frogs, and insects. Slim bodies and long tails fit them very well for jumping from branch to branch.

Why are golden lion tamarins endangered?

Their habitat is shrinking. As Rio de Janeiro spreads out, the city takes over more and more forestland, leaving less room for the tamarins. Where there are no trees, the monkeys have no food or places to rest. In addition, people capture the monkeys for zoos and private collections.

Golden lion tamarins

Are people saving the monkeys?

Yes. As a last resort, people began raising many kinds of endangered monkeys in captivity in the 1980s. Zookeepers ran into a special problem with the golden lion tamarins. The monkeys refused to mate in zoos. After much study, the keepers discovered that the tamarins prefer small spaces and little groups. Now the tamarins mate and give birth.

Keepers often hide the animals' food high up on branches in the cage. This teaches the zoo-raised monkeys how to climb trees and search for food in the wild.

When the monkeys are grown, the scientists fly them to Brazil. They release them into a huge rain forest reserve that the government has set aside. The land provides the tamarins with the habitat they need to survive. So far, the program seems to be working. Golden lion tamarins are making a comeback.

Where have all the tigers gone?

From the jungles, woods, grasslands, and swamps of Asia—to near extinction. Today, there are fewer than 5,000 tigers in all of Asia.

A tiger is a great solitary hunter. Its brownish-yellow coat with black stripes hides it in wooded or grassy surroundings. Here it waits to pounce on any deer, wild pigs, wild oxen, or monkeys that come near.

Tigers are the largest members of the cat family. An adult can weigh 500 pounds (226.8 kg) or more and stretches about 10 feet (3 m) from head to tail. Almost always hungry, an average-size tiger eats about 50 large animals a year. A mother tiger with cubs needs even more prey—perhaps 70 prey animals a year.

Why are tigers endangered?

People are moving into the tigers' habitat. Villagers living in or near where tigers live have cut down jungles and woods for farms and homes. They've drained the swamps and dug up grasslands to grow crops. To feed themselves, the people overhunt the animals that are also the tigers' prey.

Tigers that cannot find enough prey in the wild attack cattle and other farm animals. Farmers kill or poison the tigers to protect their herds. Some even burn down the forests where the tigers live. This only makes the problem worse.

Of course, there are also the poachers. Poachers kill large numbers of tigers for their valuable skins. One tiger pelt, for a rug or wall hanging, is worth over $2,000!

Are people saving the tigers?

Yes. In 1972, the Indian government and various organizations set up "Operation Tiger." This effort preserves the tigers' habitat and protects them from poachers. The news is good. There's been a slow, small increase in the tiger population.

Bengal tiger

Black rhinoceroses

Where have all the rhinoceroses gone?

From the swamps and grasslands of Asia and Africa—to near extinction. Today, the number of surviving rhinos ranges from no more than 50 Javan rhinos to about 3,500 black rhinos.

Rhinos are among the largest land animals, second only to elephants. There are five species of rhinos. Three kinds live in Asia and have a single horn. The two African species have two horns growing in a row. A wounded rhino may charge a hunter or a threatening enemy. Otherwise, rhinos are harmless animals that only eat grass, twigs, and bushes.

Why are rhinos endangered?

Overhunting is the main reason. Poachers mostly shoot rhinos for their horns. They sell the ground-up horns to people who use them as medicine. Traders pay the poachers as much as $13,000 a pound (0.5 kg) for the horns. Since a black rhino's front horn can be more than 3 feet (0.9 m) long and weigh well over 1 pound (0.5 kg), this is quite a sum!

Some people make the handles for very expensive daggers from rhino horn. According to an old belief, daggers made of rhino horn are magical and protect the owners from harm. For the rhino, the belief is a disaster!

Can people save the rhinos?

Yes. But people must stop using rhino "products" for their supposedly magical properties.

Then, more countries in Africa and Asia must protect the few remaining rhinos in parks and nature reserves. So far, protection seems to be working. But it will take time before the rhinos are out of danger.

Where have all the Arabian oryx gone?

From the deserts of Arabia—to near extinction. Large herds of Arabian oryx used to roam the deserts. In October 1972, a hunter killed the very last Arabian oryx in the wild.

The Arabian oryx has a black-and-white face and two long, slightly curved horns. Very well adapted to harsh, dry conditions, the noble-looking white antelope eats small, stunted desert plants. It can go for nearly a year without drinking water.

Why are the Arabian oryx endangered?

Too many have been killed for meat and for sport. In earlier times, Arab tribesmen hunted the animals on foot or on camels and shot them with primitive rifles. But modern inventions increased the killing. As time went on, hunters followed the oryx with four-wheel-drive vehicles and used powerful automatic weapons to shoot them. Before long, the last Arabian oryx disappeared from the wild. Fortunately, a few oryx were already safe in zoos.

Are people saving the Arabian oryx?

Yes. In the early 1960s, wildlife protection groups brought four oryx to the Phoenix, Arizona zoo. The city is set in a desert area, much like the oryx's native habitat. Over the following years, the Phoenix zookeepers started a captive-breeding program.

The breeding program worked very well. The number of Arabian oryx grew quickly. In a few years, Phoenix was able to send animals to other zoos. By 1975, zoos across the country had about 100 oryx.

In 1980, United States scientists flew 14 oryx to the Middle East. For two years they kept the oryx in a 250-acre (101 ha) protected habitat. Then they released the animals into the wild. The Arabian oryx is still an endangered animal. But its numbers are climbing.

Arabian oryx

BIRDS IN TROUBLE

Where have all the bald eagles gone?

From all over North America—to near extinction. In 1782, when this bird became a symbol of the United States, there were tens of thousands of eagles throughout North America. By the 1980s, there were fewer than 1,000 left in the 48 mainland states.

Bald eagles usually build their nests in the tops of tall trees near lakes or rivers. Females generally lay one or two eggs each year. After the eggs hatch, both parents guard the nest. They feed the young until they can get their own food. Bald eagles are very good parents!

Why are bald eagles endangered?

People took over their habitats. Americans cut down many of the trees where bald eagles made their nests. Settlers built houses and farms on the land. People also hunted the birds for sport and because they believed the bald eagles preyed upon their livestock.

The chemical pesticide DDT was another major killer. Farmers used DDT to get rid of insect pests. But some of this poison washed into lakes and streams, where it was swallowed by fish. When eagles ate the fish, DDT entered their bodies. It made the shells of the eagles' eggs very thin. They broke easily. Fewer and fewer chicks hatched. Bald eagles became endangered animals.

Are people saving the bald eagles?

Yes. In 1940, the United States government passed a law that made it a crime to harm a bald eagle, its eggs, or its nest. Then, in 1972, the government outlawed the use of DDT.

This started the eagle on the long road to recovery.

Bald eagles

Where have all the California condors gone?

From both coasts of North America—to near extinction. Today, about 40 condors fly free in scattered areas along the Pacific coast and Arizona.

The biggest of all flying birds in North America, the California condor has a wingspan of about 10 feet (3 m). When looking for prey, condors soar through the air at speeds of up to 55 miles an hour (88.5 kph). Some travel as far as 140 miles (225 km) a day— flapping their wings an average of only once an hour!

Like other vultures, condors feed on the remains of dead animals. They use their scaly claws and hooked beaks to tear apart the flesh of their lifeless prey. This makes condors extremely useful. By eating dead animals, they help clean up the land.

Why are California condors endangered?

Mostly because of random killings. Hunters shot thousands and thousands of these birds. Many more were poisoned to death by eating animals shot with lead bullets. Other birds died after feeding on contaminated bait that ranchers set out to kill coyotes. A number flew head on into power lines. And many more drank water from polluted streams—and perished.

California condor

Are people saving the California condors?

Yes. In the 1960s, zoos began to collect the 60 or so condors that remained in the wild. In 1987, the last wild California condor arrived at the San Diego Zoo.

Over the next few years, scientists set up a mating-and-breeding program. Keepers feed the birds using a hand puppet that looks like a mother condor. This teaches the young to expect food from other condors, not from people.

When the condors are grown, the scientists release them into a protected enclosure high in the mountains of a California park. After a while, they let the birds go free. Some build nests, mate, and raise their own offspring.

But the news is not all good. About 35 of the 104 condors released by the year 2000 did not survive. The experts are still working on the problem.

Brown pelicans

Where have all the brown pelicans gone?

From the coasts of North and South America—to near extinction. By 1903, there were only a few brown pelicans left. That year, President Theodore Roosevelt created Florida's Pelican Island National Wildlife Refuge to protect them.

You can tell a brown pelican by its brown feathers and long, straight bill. Underneath the bill is a pouch for catching fish. These birds almost always hunt for food in flocks. Often they fly around until they spot a fish near the surface of the water. Then they dive down and nab it.

Pelicans also nest in large groups. Some build their homes out of twigs and other plant materials that they place on the ground. Females lay two or three eggs, which hatch in a month or so. The parents care for the young for as long as three months.

Why are brown pelicans endangered?

Mainly due to hunting. In the late 1800s and early 1900s, people killed pelicans for their feathers, which were used for women's hats and other clothing. Fishermen also killed many pelicans in the 1920s. They blamed the birds for eating too many fish.

Then DDT became a problem. Rains washed the chemical into rivers and lakes where fish absorbed the poison. Pelicans ate these fish and laid eggs that broke easily. Few chicks hatched—and the number of pelicans fell even further.

Are people saving the brown pelicans?

Yes. A series of government actions started the recovery of the brown pelican. First, the government created Pelican Island. Then, it passed a law making it a crime to shoot pelicans. In 1972, a ruling banned the use of DDT. The Endangered Species Act a year later further protected the bird.

The number of brown pelicans in the wild is going up. Soon these birds may be removed from the endangered list. That will be a happy day!

Where have all the whooping cranes gone?

From wetland habitats in North America—to near extinction. In the 1940s, the total population of whooping cranes was down to only 20.

Often called whoopers, whooping cranes live in remote, marshy areas. Their name comes from their loud, trumpetlike cries. Pairs of male and female whoopers build their nests in shallow water. They pile grass, weeds, and other plants into a mound. Then the female crane usually lays two eggs—even though the parents only care for one chick.

Why are whooping cranes endangered?

People have destroyed their wetland habitat. Each whooper family needs about 400 acres (162 ha) of wetland. But as the country grew, settlers drained marshes and swamps to make room for pastures and farmland. This drove the whoopers from their homes and feeding places.

Hunters also shot great numbers of birds. And many more whoopers lost their lives flying into power lines. All this put these cranes in serious danger.

Are people saving the whoopers?

Yes. Scientists know that whoopers usually lay two eggs. But the birds only hatch one of them. So the idea arose of "stealing" one egg from each whooper nest and carefully hatching them. This slowly built up flocks of these birds.

Experts also place some eggs in the nests of sandhill cranes. The sandhills hatch the whooper eggs and care for the chicks like foster parents. When grown, the whooping cranes fly off and mate with other whoopers.

Migrating flocks of whoopers can now fly to safe havens in the United States and Canada. One flock spends every winter at the Aransas National Wildlife Refuge in a Texas coastal swamp. And every spring the whoopers head north to hatch their eggs in Canada's Wood Buffalo National Park. These reserves are helping to save the whoopers.

Whooping cranes

Where have all the snail kites gone?

From Florida, especially the large swampy area called the Everglades—to near extinction. The Everglade snail kite once inhabited large stretches of freshwater marshes throughout Florida. Today, it lives only in nine small areas of the state. At last count, there were only about 300 birds in the wild.

The blue-black bird is a kind of hawk with broad wings and a long, thin, hooked bill. It is closely related to 20 other kinds of kites. Most feed on frogs, lizards, snakes, and insects. But the snail kite eats only one kind of animal—a freshwater snail called the Florida apple snail. The kite hooks its bill into the shell's opening and pulls out the snail.

Snail kites

Why are Everglade snail kites endangered?

They lost their food supply. Starting in 1906, the government of Florida wanted to provide more farmland for its growing population. So the state drained, or dried up, large areas of the Everglades to raise sugarcane, vegetables, and other crops. The drop in water level had an unexpected effect. It killed off the apple snails—the snail kite's only food. Without snails to feed on, the snail kite became an endangered species.

Are people saving the Everglade snail kites?

Yes, by working to restore the freshwater marshes. In 1983, the state and federal governments started a program to channel water back into some drained areas. This allowed the apple snails to multiply. In time, we hope to see flocks of snail kites return to this part of Florida.

Where have all the warblers gone?

From North and South America—to near extinction. Warblers spend the summers in various places around the United States and Canada. They find the insects they eat in forests, parks, along streams, and even in trees growing in big cities.

When cold winter weather comes, many warblers fly south to tropical rain forests in South and Central America. And that's where they run into trouble. Huge tracts of these rain forests have been cut down or destroyed. The warblers cannot find their winter homes. Many die and never return north in the spring. The Seychelles warbler is one kind of warbler. It has a special problem.

Seychelles warblers

Why are Seychelles warblers endangered?

People have destroyed their habitat on Cousin Island in the Indian Ocean. It is the only place where these birds live.

For many years, Seychelles warblers found their food and made their nests in Cousin Island's bushes and low trees. Then, settlers arrived on the island. They planted many big, tall coconut palm trees. As the palms grew and spread, they took over much of the land. The palms forced out the scrubland that was the warbler's natural habitat. As a result, by the 1960s there were only about 30 Seychelles warblers left in the world!

Are people saving the Seychelles warblers?

Yes. People on Cousin Island have cut down many coconut palms. This allows the bushes and low trees to grow back. The number of warblers is starting to rise on Cousin Island. You will still find the Seychelles warbler on the list of endangered animals. But this lovely bird seems to be making a comeback.

Where have all the piping plovers gone?

From their habitats along the Atlantic and Gulf coasts—to near extinction.

Piping plovers are shorebirds that are different from most birds that live at the edge of the sea. Plovers do not dig in the sand for their food. They find their food—insects, worms, and crabs—on the surface. The female usually lays four spotted eggs in a nest that she builds on the sand.

Why are piping plovers endangered?

People destroy their nests. Unfortunately, humans and plovers use the same beaches during the birds' nesting season. People often accidentally step on the eggs, which look like pebbles in the sand. Also, more off-road vehicles travel along beaches. They crush the plover nests, eggs, and chicks under their tires. Sometimes, the drivers don't even know it! Building beach homes along the shore is another problem.

Are people saving the piping plovers?

Yes. People are working to protect the beaches in the spring. Some towns surround plover nesting areas with fences to keep people out. Others ban vehicles from the beaches.

Staying away from the plovers while they're hatching their eggs and raising their chicks helps a great deal. It means that one day these birds will grace our shores again.

Piping plovers and nest

WATER ANIMALS IN TROUBLE

Where have all the great whales gone?

From the oceans of the world—to near extinction. People have hunted these whales for more than 1,000 years. In the last century alone, hunters killed about 18,000 great whales every year!

Whales can be divided into two groups. One group has teeth; the other does not. Instead, the second group has baleen, which looks like hundreds of long, skinny fingernails hanging from their upper jaws. The baleen acts like a built-in strainer. It filters tiny creatures out of the seawater that the whales take into their mouths.

Are toothed whales endangered?

Yes—especially the sperm whale, the biggest toothed whale by far. During the 1800s, it was the most hunted toothed whale.

The sperm whale's enormous boxlike head makes up a huge part of its body. It contains a large supply of oil used to make candles and face creams. From the skull of each male sperm whale, whalers collected about 10 barrels of this valuable product.

Whalers also looked for ambergris (AM-bur-grees), a waxy substance found in the intestines of some sperm whales. Workers add ambergris to expensive perfumes to make the odor last longer.

Why are baleen whales endangered?

Whalers hunted these whales for the strong, light, elastic baleen, which is also called whalebone. Manufacturers used whalebone to make umbrellas, fishing rods, buggy whips, and hoop skirts.

Sperm whale

Blue whale

Which baleen whales are in greatest danger?

The blue, bowhead, humpback, gray, and right whales.

Blue whales are the biggest animals that ever lived. Yet, despite their huge size, they feed entirely on krill, tiny shrimplike creatures that they filter from the water. Few blue whales swim the oceans anymore. Their future looks bleak.

Bowhead whales also strain krill from the water. They have the longest baleen of any whale. Once common in nearly all arctic waters, bowheads are now rarely seen.

Humpback whales do not have humps on their backs. They got this name from the way they hump, or show their back when they dive. But they do have some of the longest flippers of any whale. These whales used to swim along the coasts. Today, they're nearly all gone.

Gray whales once swam in both the Atlantic and Pacific oceans. Now you can only find them in the Pacific. At two different times, gray whales almost disappeared. But each time, they came back. Today, these great whales seem to be doing well.

Right whales got their name from hunters who said they were the "right" whales to hunt. They swim slowly and close to shore, float when killed, and provide large amounts of oil and baleen. As a result, hunters went after them. Their numbers remain small.

Can people save the whales?

Yes. In 1946, the major whaling countries formed the International Whaling Commission (IWC). Its job was to protect whales from being overhunted. They also passed regulations controlling the whaling industry. The IWC later set limits on the numbers of each species of whale that could be killed. It also banned the hunting of certain kinds of whales.

Ending ocean pollution is another way to save whales. Poisons and garbage in the water destroy the whales' food supply. It also ruins many of the places where whales mate and give birth. Although much hunted, most species of whales may survive after all.

Where have all the manatees gone?

From waters in the southeastern United States, the Caribbean Sea, and along the west coast of Africa—to near extinction.

Manatees are large, friendly-looking mammals that feed on plants they find in the water. Sometimes called "sea cows" because of their diet, manatees spend five to eight hours a day eating. Most adult manatees are about 10 feet (3 m) long and weigh between 800 and 1,200 pounds (363 and 544 kg). Some can be longer than 12 feet (3.6 m) long and weigh 3,500 pounds (1,600 kg).

Why are manatees endangered?

During the nineteenth century, people killed tremendous numbers of manatees, mainly for food. They called the very tasty manatee meat "sea beef." Workers also melted the heavy layer of blubber, or fat, from the manatee to make an oil widely used in cooking. And people found many uses for the thick, strong manatee skin.

Today, the major threat to manatees is power boats. Power boats have propeller blades that can slash the slow-moving manatees. Sometimes the blades kill the manatee immediately. More often, they wound the animal, leaving it to die slowly. Manatees that survive usually have huge scars on their backs from collisions with motorboats.

Also, pollution kills the sea grasses that manatees eat. Without grasses, manatees starve to death.

Are people saving the manatees?

Yes. Cleaning up the waters by stopping pollution is one important way people can help. The second way is by controlling power boats. The U.S. Navy puts metal cages around the propellers of tugboats that travel in manatee waters. Naval officers find that the cages keep the manatees away from the spinning blades. Some experts think the manatees are slowly coming back.

Manatees

Where have all the sea otters gone?

From the North Pacific Ocean—to near extinction. Sea otters off the coast of California were nearly all gone by the year 1929. Most survivors now live off the coast of Alaska. Only a few can be found along the California seacoast.

Sea otters are furry mammals that are about the size and weight of 12-year-old kids. These playful, affectionate, gentle animals live in family groups. The parents raise the young, usually a single pup at a time. On land, the mother carries the pup in her mouth. But when they are in the water, she swims on her back with the pup resting on her belly.

Before going to sleep at night, sea otters often wrap themselves in the tall brown kelp that grows up from the ocean floor. The sleeping otters then float on their backs. The wrapping keeps them from being carried away by waves or tides. At dawn, the otters dive down to the ocean floor to find clams, crabs, or oysters in the kelp forest. Each carries a small stone in its front paws to crack open its shellfish dinner!

Sea otters

Why are sea otters endangered?

Many were killed for their beautiful, thick brown fur. Pollution, too, claimed many lives. The numbers of sea otters went way down. Without otters to eat them, sea urchins multiplied. Sea urchins destroyed much of the plant growth along that coast. This left little food or hiding places for fish and other sea creatures. Their numbers dropped, too.

From 1969 to 1972, scientists released 100 otters born elsewhere into waters off California. In a short time, the count of sea urchins fell. The amount of fish and other creatures in the waters rose. The balance of life began to be restored.

On March 24, 1989, the oil tanker *Exxon Valdez* slammed into a rock off the coast of Alaska. It spilled about 11 million gallons of crude oil into the frigid waters. This single spill claimed the lives of about 5,500 sea otters.

Are people saving sea otters?

Yes. In 1911, several nations signed a treaty banning the hunting of sea otters. Since then the population has been growing steadily. You can now see numbers of these animals in more areas along the Pacific coast. Recent protection and reintroduction programs also seem to be bringing back the sea otters.

Where have all the sea turtles gone?

From warm seas around the world—to near extinction. This includes six of the seven species—green turtle, hawksbill, loggerhead, Kemp's ridley, olive ridley, and leatherback.

Sea turtles spend their entire lives in the sea. But the female sea turtle comes up on land to lay her eggs. She lays about 100 eggs in her nest every two weeks during the season. The female drags herself up on the beach, buries her eggs, and rushes back to the water as quickly as she can. When the eggs hatch, the defenseless newborns dash across the beach to the water. Raccoons, gulls, crabs, dogs, and other animals catch most of the baby turtles, called hatchlings, before they reach the sea. Usually, only 1 out of every 100 survives.

Why are sea turtles endangered?

For several reasons. Nesting and hatchling sea turtles find their way by moonlight and its reflection on the water. But beaches with artificial lights confuse the turtles and their young. They often get lost following these lights.

Before the days of refrigeration, sailors caught sea turtles and kept them alive on their ships. This gave the crew a supply of fresh meat during long voyages. It also seriously reduced the numbers of sea turtles. Traders around the world still catch turtles for food. They also use their shells and fat to make various products.

Oil spills and water pollution claim many lives, too. A number of young sea turtles have choked to death on big gobs of heavy black tar formed from oil dumped in the ocean. Garbage is a particular danger. Not long ago, one dead turtle was found with strands of plastic rope, a plastic balloon, parts of a plastic bottle, a plastic comb, and a plastic flower in its stomach!

Are people saving the sea turtles?

Yes. Fishermen are protecting sea turtles by using special nets. These allow the sea turtles to escape if accidentally caught while the fishermen are trawling for shrimp.

There is also another important way people save sea turtles. During the nesting season, people shut off artificial lights near the hatchling areas. This helps turtles keep safe while nesting. It also lets them use light from the moon to find their way to the sea.

Green sea turtle

Where have all the alligators and crocodiles gone?

From the banks of warm rivers, lakes, and swamps—to near extinction.

Alligators and crocodiles are almost look-alikes. Both have narrow bodies, rough skins, short legs, and long tails. But alligators have wide snouts; crocodile snouts come more to a point. Alligators move more slowly than crocodiles.

In the winter, American alligators rest in deep water-filled holes that they dig in the soft mud. During periods of drought, or dry periods, these "'gator holes" are good hiding places for fish, frogs, turtles, and snails. Without alligators to dig these holes, animals that need water to survive may die.

Crocodiles are also very important in Africa. These endangered animals feed on great numbers of so-called trash fish that live in lakes and rivers. This leaves more food fish for the people who depend on them. Fewer crocodiles mean more trash fish. Trash fish force out the food fish—and the people go hungry.

American alligators

Why are alligators and crocodiles endangered?

Food, fun, farming, and fashion claim many lives. People eat alligator and crocodile meat and eggs. Hunters shoot these powerful beasts for sport. Workers drain the swamps and streams in which the alligators and crocodiles live to make room for farms. And traders kill many alligators and crocodiles for their skins—mainly to make handbags, shoes, belts, and briefcases.

Are people saving the American alligators?

Yes. Since the 1950s, the United States has passed laws banning the killing of American alligators. These laws work very well. By 1987, these animals had made a remarkable recovery. In some areas, there were even too many alligators. People in parts of Florida and Louisiana complained of alligators in their yards and swimming pools!

Today, American alligators are not endangered, but they are threatened. They still do need our protection.

Have any animals come back from near extinction?

Several have. The peregrine falcon is an outstanding example of a recovered endangered species. At last count, there were an estimated 1,650 breeding pairs of peregrine falcons in the United States and Canada.

Like other birds of prey, peregrine falcons hunt and kill other animals for food. Normally, they dive to catch doves, ducks, and other birds in midair. On such dives, their speeds may reach more than 200 miles an hour (320 kph)! Few fast-flying birds can top this record.

Why were peregrine falcons endangered?

Most were killed by the pesticide DDT. This deadly chemical got into the falcons' bodies through their food. Peregrine falcons fed on birds that preyed on insects killed by DDT. When the falcons ate these birds, the DDT entered the falcons' systems.

The DDT caused the females to lay eggs with thin shells. When the birds sat on the eggs, the shells collapsed, and the unhatched chicks died.

How did people save the peregrine falcons?

In two main ways. In the 1970s, the United States and some other countries banned the use of DDT. This started the peregrine falcon on the way to recovery.

Captive-breeding programs also helped. Scientists in various governmental and private organizations mated pairs of falcons. The birds successfully hatched thousands of young. Since 1974, scientists have released more than 6,000 birds into the wild. In August 1999, authorities removed the peregrine falcon from the list of endangered animals.

Many large cities now have peregrine falcons. Often, they build their nests on top of skyscrapers or high bridges. The falcons prey on pigeons and other city birds. The peregrine falcons are back in good numbers. It is a great success story.

Peregrine falcons and nest

How can I help?

There are several ways. You can—

- write to state fish-and-game or natural resources departments to find out what species are endangered in your area.
- visit any wildlife refuges or fish hatcheries near where you live.
- become a volunteer at a refuge or hatchery.
- be a good recycler; avoid unnecessary use of pesticides and herbicides, and dispose of trash properly.
- participate in animal counts or online reporting of animal activity.

Why is it important to save endangered animals?

Each species plays a part in the balance of life. The loss of any species threatens the survival of other living things.

Thousands of species of animals are presently in danger. And the number grows bigger each year. The loss of large numbers of different animals harms everyone, including humans.

Until recently, an animal species died out, or became extinct, largely because of natural causes. For example, a change in climate probably caused the extinction of the mammoths. But today, most animals become endangered because of what people do. The clearing of wild areas, illegal hunting, and pollution make it very difficult for many animals to survive.

It's time for us to change our ways.

Bald eagle

INDEX

Africa   9, 15, 36
Alaska   38
alligators   4, 42 – 43
apple snails   27
Arabia   16
Arabian oryx   16 – 17
Aransas National Wildlife Refuge 24
Asia   12, 15
Atlantic coast   30
bald eagles   3, 4, 18 – 19
beach nests   30 –31, 40 – 41
birds   18 – 31
boat propellers   36
Brazil   10, 11
brown pelicans   3, 4, 22 – 23
California   38
California condors   3, 20 – 21
Canada   24, 44
captive breeding 4, 6, 11, 17, 21, 45
Caribbean Sea   36
chemicals   18
China   6
Cousin Island   29
crocodiles   3, 42 – 43
crops   27
DDT   18, 23, 44
dinosaurs   3
Endangered Species Act   4, 23
endangered species list   4
Everglades   26 – 27
feathers   23

fishing nets   41
Florida   26, 43
fur   6, 39
garbage   35, 40
giant pandas   3, 6 – 7
golden lion tamarin   10 – 11
green sea turtles   5, 40 – 41
Gulf coast   30
hand feeding   21
horns   15
hunters   9, 16, 18, 20, 23
  24, 32, 35, 43
Ice Age   3
International Whaling Commission 35
land animals   6 – 17
land clearing   6, 9, 10, 12, 18, 24,
  27, 28, 43
laws   4, 18, 23, 43
logging   9
mammoths   3, 46
manatees   36 – 37
Middle East   17
migration   28
monkeys   10 – 11
mountain gorillas   3, 8 – 9
North America   18, 20, 23, 24, 28
North Pacific Ocean   38
oil spills   39, 40
overhunting 3, 12, 15, 16, 20, 23, 35
pandas, see giant pandas   39, 40

Pelican Island National
  Wildlife Refuge   23
peregrine falcons   4, 44 – 45
piping plover   30 – 31
poachers   6, 9, 10, 12, 15
poison   12, 18, 20, 23, 35
pollution   3, 20, 35, 36, 39, 40
power lines   20, 24
recovery programs   6, 9, 11, 12, 15,
  17, 18, 21, 23, 24, 27, 30, 35, 36,
  39, 43, 45
refuges/reserves   4, 6, 9, 11, 15, 21,
  23, 24
rhinoceros   14 – 15
San Diego Zoo   6, 21
sea otters   38 – 39
sea turtles   3, 40 – 41
skins   6, 12, 36, 43
snail kites   26 – 27
South America   23, 28
sperm whales   32 –33
threatened animals   3
tigers   3, 12 – 13
United States   4, 6, 18, 24, 36, 44
warblers   28 – 29
water animals   32 – 43
whales   3, 32 – 35
  baleen   32, 34 – 35
  toothed   32 – 33
whooping cranes   24 – 25
zoos   9, 10, 11, 16, 17, 21

About the Authors

Melvin and Gilda Berger live in a beachfront community where rapid home-building is endangering or threatening the lives of many kinds of animals. Through their writing and work with various organizations, the Bergers are striving to improve the outlook for endangered species everywhere.

About the Illustrator

Jim Effler was interested in illustrating this book because he hopes it will encourage kids and adults to help preserve life on Earth. He says, "The many species of endangered animals and plants help make up the balance and beauty of our planet."